A Field of Memories

mm God Bless you!

[signature]

purchased @ Katie's Sandwich Shop
11/6/2020 Sandy Run SC

A FIELD OF
Memories

Matthew Rucker

This publication contains the opinions and ideas of its author. It is intended to provide helpful and informative material on the subjects addressed in the publication. The author and publisher specifically disclaim all responsibility for any liability, loss, or risk, personal or otherwise, which is incurred as a consequence, directly or indirectly, of the use and application of any of the contents of this book.

ISBN 978-1-952405-62-4   [Paperback Edition]
          978-1-952405-61-7   [eBook Edition]

Printed and bound in The United States of America.

Published by
The Mulberry Books, LLC.
8330 E Quincy Avenue,
Denver CO 80237
themulberrybooks.com

CONTENTS

ACKNOWLEDGEMENTS

Let me first thank my dear wife, Angela, who encouraged me to write. Without her I couldn't have written this book. Also let me thank my family, friends and church members who provided the stories. Let me also thank my daughter, Rachael, who provided the picture for the book cover.

INTRODUCTION

My life has always revolved around stories. At an early age of life, I listened to my uncles as they told stories. As I grew older in life, my own stories developed. These stories have shaped me into who I am today. I try to give insight into my life, my love of God and my love of people. They also give an insight into the fact that I was a bit of a rascal. Each story is about a true event in my life that I learned from. Giving a moral at the end of the story tries to help you, the reader, gain insight into your life as well. The stories will consist of the happy and sad periods of living. So enjoy the book and who knows you may learn something about yourself.

TWO STRIKES AND YOU ARE OUT

*T*he churches in the area formed a softball league and we were involved. A team was formed and each member got a jersey and hat. My jersey had 'Preacher' written on the back. No one wanted to pitch so they nominated me.

Now, I had played softball before but never pitched. So I became the pitcher. Practice was on Monday evenings and everyone showed up. I practiced with the catcher before a batter stepped in. Warmed up, I was ready. The first batter hit one of those dribblers off to my left. I charged the ball and planted my foot to catch the ball. All of a sudden, I felt pain right away in my foot and couldn't put weight on it.

Couple of the members took me to the emergency room and found out I had split one of the bones in my foot. A cast was placed on my foot and I was out for the season before the first game. I would be back the next year. "Hang in there preacher", the teammates responded.

Spring came again and everyone began to talk about getting started with practice. It was scheduled for Monday night. When we gathered I was promoted to catcher, a position I had played in school. No problem, this year I was ready. Taking my position I turned my hat around and put on the face mask. "Let's get started", I said slapping my glove.

The first pitch went wide. So did the second. Now the third was a hittable ball and the batter swung. It ended up being a foul tip ball coming to me. The problem with a foul tip is that it is spinning at about five hundred miles an hour when it hits the glove. I misjudged the ball and it caught me on the pinkie finger snapping the ligaments in it. "Time out, Preacher is down again", the pitcher cried out.

So my second season ended in the first game. Oh I could have played the following year, but as I looked at my crooked finger, I said, "No". No telling what might have happen the next time.

Sometimes you have to have the good sense to know when to stop. Some people don't and dig themselves into a deeper hole. Knowing when to stop is wisdom. That is true in all things. You need to know when to stop teasing or making fun for a good time. Everyone needs to know when to let someone go and say 'Goodbye'.

You can go for the third strike, but you better be careful. I have found it better to quit on the second strike when things are not getting better. Ask God for wisdom to know when to sit down.

PANTS DROP DOWN

*I*t was a typical Sunday morning as I sat in my office going over my sermon. This was a regular Sunday morning ritual. At ten minutes till I would meet the choir to have prayer and then we would go in the sanctuary together.

On this Sunday as I got ready to meet the choir one of my suspender buttons popped off. So I took the suspenders off, because they were worthless. My wife spies the missing suspenders and announces that my pants will fall down. Now I assured her that everything would be fine but she wouldn't let it go. "Your pants are going to fall down", she remarked. The whole choir is standing there listening to us. I insisted that they wouldn't fall so I had to prove it to her. I reached up into the air and she was right, my pants fell down. I hate it when she is right!

It was one of my fastest moves pulling them back up, but I had lost the choir. We entered the sanctuary with the choir hiding their faces. I knew I would never get control if I let it go, so I confessed to the church what had happened.

We had a short service that Sunday and I don't think the church has ever laughed that much.

Always listen to what others may tell you. What they may be saying could be right. But you see I knew best so I turned on deaf ears. When you fail to at least listen you make a fool of yourself as I did when my pants fell down. By the way, my grandmother always told us to put on clean underwear. Well, I am just thankful I had some on when my pants fell down.

RAT AT EPWORTH

*E*very summer we went to camp meeting at Epworth. I went to camp as a counselor. They put us in individual rooms with a bunk bed. There was no air conditioning only a fan if you brought one. Believe it or not but South Carolina gets hot in June and July.

It was check in so I got my room and a set of sheets and a pillow. Made up the bottom bunk and after supper I would enjoy a humid and mid ninety night. I pray the fan doesn't quit.

After devotions we headed to our rooms and the kids to their dorms. By the way the dorm was open air as well. Lights were out at 10:00 and a big full moon shown over the camp. I left my door open to catch a breeze if one came through. Covered by only a sheet I settled in for a nights rest. All of a sudden something fell out the top mattress and under my sheet it went. I could feel him alongside my leg so I froze. I had no idea of what was in my bed with me. I lay grave yard dead waiting for escape. What seemed like eternity it finally jumped on the floor and in the moonlight I saw one of those big barn rats. So goes my goodnight sleep.

My dear friends if this had happened to some people they would be dead. I don't know how you would have fared. I did throw the top mattress out and closed my door the rest of camp. I tried to eliminate the problem. Things will happen in this life to you. Some will be surprises but think about it and try to prevent it happening again. So sleep good tonight and if you are in bunk beds check the one above you. Who knows there may be a rat in it? Sleep well!

COW AND APPLE TREE

I don't know who came up with the idea my brother or I to lasso a cow. We had this half grown cow which was about five hundred pounds and that would be our target. We had practiced throwing the lasso when in fact we could have just walked up to her and put it around her neck. I am chosen as the roper and also because I weighed more than my brother. As I told him, "Let a man do this job".

It was time so I entered the pasture. Now there was one apple tree in the middle of the field. Step one lasso the cow and then the plan would unfold before me. The cow is looking at me as I twirled the rope and then threw it. It sailed high into the air and dropped perfectly around her neck.

Now that crazy cow had never had that happen so she took off out across the pasture. Step two, since we were heading for the apple tree, I was to get there first. I could wrap the rope around the tree and she would be mine. With the encouragement of my brother shouting, "Hold her brother", I focused on the tree.

This situation had to be perfect to accomplish my plan. The tree was right in front of me and I tried to run around it. A problem which I had not worked on was the running out of rope. The rope tightens and slammed me into the tree.

When I finally figured out where I was and who I was the cow was grazing with the rope around her neck. Stumbling over to her I slipped the rope off her neck. My roping days ended as quickly as they got started.

Readers, use your head not your ego to do things in life. Don't let your ego overload your ability. Think things through. I have learned that with life. I try to allow for what may go wrong. If you don't use your head you could end up with a rope and a run a way cow on it.

MY LAST GUINEA FOWL

When I retired back to the home place, I wanted to get some guineas. My dad always liked to have them around the farm, so I decided to purchase seventeen guineas. But in this life there is always something out to get what you have. So coyotes, hawks and owls began to catch my guineas. After a while I only had one left.

Now this guinea began to stay with the cows. When they lay down this guinea would pick flies off them. He would stay with the cows all day and come to roost at night. Now that was the problem, where he chose to roost. He chose a place above my tractor in the shed. This wasn't going to work. So for many weeks I tried to make him find another place. This was a battle I was going to win. At the time the score was guinea fifty and Matt zero. Something had to be done so I got my gun and would try and scare him, but he was a sneaky little thing sneaking by me under the cover of darkness. Matt had reached his limit, and the next time I will shoot at him.

We begin the same ritual the next night but this time I saw him trying to sneak by. He raised his head and I fired. He began to flop around in the tall grass, then stillness. I hated to do it but this had to stop.

I confessed to my wife what I had done. I really did feel bad. Next morning I got up and went to feed the chickens and who greets me, the guinea. His head was bloody but eating and alive and well. I told God at that moment I would not try and hurt this guinea again. I was true to my word.

By the way the guinea became too brave. He would run at me with his wings up, which was a defensive stance. I would like to say the guinea is well but he learned you can't run at a fox and be safe.

My friends, there are dangers out in the world. Things you can't play with without getting hurt. Alcohol, drugs and sex can hurt you, even destroy you. You see the guinea thought he could handle that fox but the fox got him. Don't play around with these things that can hurt you.

NO COMMUNICATION

While in seminary a group of us went to Miami to do a church service. Hugh and I would be staying together at the hosts grandparents. Now Hugh is from Tennessee and has a long drawl when he talks. We arrived at the home where we are staying and it was nice, but the couple was from Germany and couldn't speak English. Saying hello was not a problem but everything else was.

Now Hugh felt if he just talked slow enough they would understand. They would just look at him. The grandson showed up and helped us to get what we would need during the stay.

Communication is so important and society is losing it. People communicate by texting these days. Some people will look at you but you know they are looking through you and not hearing. It's difficult for people to lay the phones down and just talk. They have lost that art. My job in the ministry was to help people find communication skills again. Many times it was like Hugh, me, and the German grandparents. Put your phone down and talk to someone, get to know them, and make a friend. You can't do that by texting.

SNAKE IN THE BALE

Every summer while in high school I would help the local dairy farmer, Roger bale hay. We would start midmorning and go until dark. My job was to throw the hay bales up onto the wagon. The wagon was hooked to the baler and as the bales came up I would throw them back to be stacked.

The stackers were two fellows that could really stack. It was a pretty boring day to say the least. But on this day things were about to happen. I spied a large black snake crawl into the row of hay. The baler picks him up and he is baled into the bale. About six inches of his head is exposed and he is wants to bite something. I should note that the snake was not poisonous.

Now the devilishness in me comes out. I threw the bale up (with the snake in it) and I hear a scream and both guys jump off the top of the bales that had been stacked on the wagon. Roger stops the tractor to find out what happened. All they could say was that there was a snake in the bale.

They wouldn't get back on the wagon to get the bale. I climb up and threw it down. I had to act surprised or they would have never trusted me again. After a break they get back on the wagon with a new attitude, but watching each bale. By the way each wagon stacked would hold one hundred twenty bales.

Be careful playing jokes on people. Those guys jumped from about fifteen foot up in the air. They could have gotten hurt. I found out they were also scared of snakes. It was funny at the time but afterwards I had to lie which was not good. There is always a downside to a joke. Someone could get hurt, so be careful with a snake in a bale.

IT'S JUST KETCHUP

My cousin, Eddie, doesn't like tomatoes in any form. He would always look for the tomatoes in his food. One night at a friend's house several of us were there and they were drinking beer. I didn't drink because to me beer will gag a maggot. My drink of choice was coke or Pepsi. After a while the conversation turned to what each of us liked to eat.

Now, Eddie doesn't like tomatoes but he said he did. You see beer will make you do crazy things. Nathen says, "No you don't like tomatoes". Eddie responds, "Yes I do, hand me that bottle of ketchup and I will show you". Now he turned that bottle up and drank the whole thing and got another beer.

The beer was running low so we went to Mr. Charlie's store for more. I drove of course. When we drive up Eddie's mom and dad are there and they see us. By now Eddie is sick and throwing up and it's as red as can be. My aunt screams, "He is hemorrhaging Edward, we have to get him to the hospital!" They soon realized that he was drunk so they captured him and drove away in the dark. Later, I heard from my aunt and I remember her words, "You should have been more responsible".

I'm not going to tell you don't drink or do drugs because it may only encourage you to do it in secret. All I'm going to say is be real careful. They can hurt you, ruin your life and destroy relationships. I have heard some people say in counseling, "I know I had a good time because people told me, but I can't remember a thing". Drugs and drinking will make you macho, super human but most of all stupid. It can make you drink even a bottle of ketchup when you don't even like it. Be careful, very careful.

HUGH AT DRUG STORE

*H*ugh had a room in the dorm at seminary across the hall from me. Now, I could tell if he had something on his mind. He would come over and stand around and chew his nails. "What do you need?" I asked him. "I feel embarrassed to tell you," he responded. "No, what can I do to help you?" I added. "Well I'm constipated and I need a suppository and I don't want go in the drug store and ask for one," he said. "Come on," I said, "I'll help you out".

We got in my car and headed to the drug store. He kept thanking me for the help. Arriving at the drug store a small crowd was waiting on the druggist. Finally, she looked at us and says, "How can I help you?" I responded pointing to Hugh, "He needs a suppository".

As we left he told me that if he knew I was going to do what I did he would have taken care of it. Later on that night we laughed about it.

Friends play tricks on friends, but not to hurt. Let me add that Hugh is a friend that won't try to hurt you, but got me on several occasions. Hugh and I are good friends and he too has retired from the ministry. I love him to death and would do anything I could for him. Maybe the way I handled it wasn't the best way but Hugh got relief.

NEILL AND HERBERT

*N*eill and Herbert were members of a church I served. I became very close to them because of Herbert's health. He was in and out of the hospital so there were many visits to their home and hospital.

On one occasion Neill called to say Herbert was not doing well at all. He was in the hospital and could I go and see him. I told her "yes" and I would be up in a little bit to visit. When I arrived at his room he and Neill were the only ones in the room.

We talked a while and then I said, "Let's have prayer". We held hands and I prayed for them. I asked for healing for Herbert and comfort for Neill. As I closed the prayer I said, "Lord, bless Hell and Nerbert". Their hands began to shake and I thought this is a good prayer and God is doing something. I said a few more things and closed with "Amen". When I did they both busted out laughing. "What happened", I said. "You don't realize it but you asked God to bless Hell and Nerbert", Neill added. We all laughed together after that statement.

I think the laughter helped them both. By the way I used that story at Herbert's funeral. It always remained a special time for Neill and me.

God works in mysterious ways and he used my tongue twister to bring joy. I believe this is what they both needed, to laugh. Sometimes you can say something wrong and God can use it. Something as simple as switching the first letter of Neill and Herbert.

FIRST BLACK WEDDING

My wife informed me that we had been invited to a co-worker's wedding. It was held on the edge of a pond in June with a mosquito convention going on. We arrived and they sat us in chairs on the bride's side. As I sat there waiting for the wedding to start a young lady said, "Reverend Rucker, you need to sit up there because you are helping with the service". I turned to my wife and gave her a look and she responded, "I didn't know!"

So I move up closer to the pond and the mosquitos were singing in harmony. Now the wedding started late, about two hour late and those mosquitoes enjoyed me during that time.

The other ministers gathered with me and I asked them, "What I was supposed to do?" They looked at me and said, "We thought you would tell us". So in the dark holding flashlights we got it done. Everyone was happy!

Reader, I told you there are lots of surprises in life. Don't lose it but square your shoulders and do the best you can. Oh, always pray before you do anything. Knowing me you should know that I like things prepared and don't like to fly by the seat of my pants. But I had to make the most out of this situation. It was my first black wedding and it has become one of my favorite memories. By the way I don't miss those mosquitoes, they ate me alive. Get ready for those surprises of life and remember you can handle them.

SNAKE IN NEW MEXICO

I took a mission team of twelve to the Indian Reservation in New Mexico. We were to work on a church. As with each mission trip the people inform us of customs and practices but also dangerous concerns. Now, in New Mexico the biggest dangers are the rattlesnakes. They are everywhere and they come out at night to lie on the roads. Now this was hammered into to us to be careful.

Our living quarters were this big counsel room where they had their meetings and we slept on the floor on pallets. We settled in for the first night. That first night we had this fellow that snored and one team member moved his bed into the hall. Now I had to go to the bathroom in the middle of the night and I didn't want to wake Billy up in the hall.

So I didn't turn any lights on. Feeling my way around the hall I approached the bathroom. It is dark and all of a sudden I stepped on something that rolled under my foot. I jumped straight up and came down on it again. I jumped again thinking 'rattlesnake'. This time I was against the wall with nothing under my feet. I froze for if I moved the snake will get me. I stood there for eternity it seemed and then the lights came on.

One of the girls had to use the bathroom. I looked down and there on the floor was a water hose that someone pulled across the floor to water something outside. I must confess I thought of a lot of things to say but I bit my tongue. I do know this that was the only time I felt I ever was going to have a heart attack.

Have you ever been scared, really scared? If not it will come. Try not to let your mind create the story. I had been lectured about the snakes and when I stepped on the hose it had to be a snake. Try to remain calm as you can and don't try to do a lot at the time. I will say this, if you had stepped on that hose in the dark you would have screamed 'snake'.

MY FIRST CRUISE

My wife and I went on our first cruse together. I was excited as a kid in a candy store. We boarded the ship and had a safety briefing. We had to know where to go if the ship were to sink. Being from the country my thoughts was to get to the highest point, the smoke stacks.

We then left port and sailed through the night to the islands. That day we went ashore and came back to sail that night. Finally, on the way to the next port we sailed during the day. It was called a 'day at sea'. My wife said she didn't want to lie out in the sun so she went to the spa. I grabbed my towel and off to the pool I headed.

When I got there you couldn't put another chair around the pool. Looking up I saw chairs on an upper deck so I headed up. When I arrived, no one was up on this deck. I said to myself, "This is perfect". I drug a chair out and laid down in the sun. I fell asleep.

I heard people talking around me and I woke up. Opening my eyes I see this topless lady. She say, "Hello". I said "Hello", and turned over. I'm thinking to myself 'where the heck am I'? When I turned over there were more topless ladies. They were friendly and talked with me. They drug their chairs up closes to me as we talked. I promise you I tried to maintain eye contact. "Where are you from?" one asked. I said, "South Carolina. Now I found out about their lives and what they did but I never told them I was a minister.

Now, later on one of these ladies went to the spa and got into a conversation with my wife. "Where are you from?" she asked. Her answer was South Carolina. She said, I met the nicest man up on the topless deck from South Carolina". My wife asked, "What did he look like?" She described me to a tee. My wife came looking for me. I was in the room. "What were you doing on the topless deck?" she asked me. I tried to explain that I didn't' know it was topless, that no one was up there when I got there. She could believe that happening to me.

Now, what's so funny is that I would run into these ladies on the ship and they would say, "Hello, Matt?" "Who was that?" my wife would ask. "Oh, they are from the topless deck", I would respond.

Honest mistakes can happen in life. Most people try to talk their way out of it but the more you talk the worst it gets. I kept it simple stating the facts. If people had been there I would have turned around at once, but no one was there and I had found my private place. When you defend yourself, keep it simple. I have been on three other cruses, but have not gone up top again.

TRAINING A HAWK

*L*ife throws some interesting situations at us. Such was the time my brother and I found an 'injured' hawk. His wing was hurt, so we decided to catch him. We got an old burlap sheet and threw over him capturing him. We threw him in an old dog box.

It just so happened when we went to my aunt's house to watch TV, Wild Kingdom was on. The program dealt with falcons that will fly and kill a rabbit, quail, or dove. "Hot dog we got us something," I told my brother.

Now, the training would begin. My brother got a pair of dad's welding gloves and went to the box. Opening the door he eased his arm in for the hawk to jump on it just like on TV. We figured that would be the first step, the rest would be easy. My brother pushed his arm closer and all at once the hawk leaped on his arm. One problem, he missed the glove landing on Jimmy's bare arm.

Training was over for my brother and he grabbed the hawk by the neck and killed him. Those claws did a job on my brother, Jimmy's arm. That was the first and last hawk we tried to make into a falcon.

We all do some crazy things, each of you will too. Don't get down on yourself, learn to laugh about it. Jimmy and I felt we had a simple, easy and good plan. We didn't realize that there is always more to any plan. Think about what you're going to do before you do it. Make sure your gloves are higher when training a hawk.

WINDOW FAN FOR A/C

During these hot summer days in South Carolina I often think of my childhood. We didn't have any air conditioner, we had a window fan. The fan would be placed in a window blowing air out. At the same time each window in the house was opened about an inch. The outside air would be pulled into the house.

We went to bed in our underwear and just a sheet on the bed. Screens were on the windows to keep bugs and mosquitoes out, but every now and then a mosquito would get in. You could hear him but couldn't see him. The room wouldn't get cool till way up in the morning. By then you were wet with sweat but the rest of the night it was comfortable.

Today we have air conditioning in almost everything such as; our homes, at work, in the car, in the stores, and in our farm equipment. Sometimes I wonder how we made it back then but it was what we got used to.

Friends, you are blessed to have all the modern conveniences you have. You are cool at night when you sleep. By the way, today I sleep cool at night as well. I trust that you thank God for all these blessings everyday especially the air conditioning when it's summer in Columbia, South Carolina.

FRUIT IN HONDURAS

I took a team to Honduras on a mission trip which consisted of twelve team members. We were going to the area where Hurricane Mitch came through on the southern side. This is a remote area only assessable by Jeep. The road is very muddy and we had to drive through rivers along the way. When we arrived at our destination our quarters were a three sided building with a top.

Each trip you make to a foreign country there are safety precautions. We had to sleep under a net because of the insects and poisonous frogs. The major concern was the eating their food especially the fruit because of sanitary conditions. Now the interpreter briefs us on this each day for our safety.

The next day we begin work on laying block for a new house. It was hot and we would stop at noon and have a siesta till two. When we got back to the site some kids had a plate offering us fruit. Everyone was refusing but I couldn't break those kids' heart. I took a piece and it was good so I had another then another. They were happy and I was happy. I slept well that night.

Next morning I went out to the bathroom, a hole in the ground. I began to urinate and I notice it was bright red. I then remembered the words of the interpreter 'There are some bad germs down here'. I thought I got one and I am hemorrhaging and was dying. I needed to get on my antibodies right away. It was time for the team meeting; the interpreter again warned us about eating the food because it could really hurt you. I thought, "Yeah, I'm sitting here bleeding to death". Then someone asked him what the fruit was that the kids had at the job site. He called its name and said they use it for dye.

He laughed and said, "If you eat this fruit your pee will turn bright red". I heard the angels sing. Boy did I feel better but I didn't take any other fruit on the trip.

This did scare me when it happened but I now know that God in His mercy took care of me. Sometimes we have something blow up in our face before we learn. Remember, we learn from everything in life that affects us. Learn from it and keep on doing good. Just remember to listen to others who know, then fruit can't hurt you.

RUG TRUCKER

I was a hospital chaplain at Spartanburg Regional Medical Center for one year. This is a large hospital and my duties were vast. I had to be on call every third night and I couldn't sleep because the beeper was always going off. Most of the night involved the Emergency Department. The rest of the time was handling deaths in the hospital or helping with patients who just needed to talk. I would also try to support the staff when it was necessary.

Another area I was responsible for during the day was the Psych Unit. Patients would just want to talk with a chaplain. Such a call came to me one morning. Arriving at the unit the nurse pointed out who wanted to see me. I walked over and spoke to her. I had read her chart and she had tried to commit suicide. I asked her what her name was and she told me. Then she asked me what was my name and I showed her my badge and said, "Matt, like a rug on the floor and think of trucker and take the 'T' off and you have Rucker." "Matt Rucker", she said, "I can remember that!!" We talked awhile and then I left.

The next day I got a call to come see her again. Walking in she came to meet me. She said, "Don't tell me your name because I remember it, Rug Trucker". I smiled and said, "Yeah that's me". The staff picked up on it and soon it seemed the whole hospital knew. People would speak to me and say "Hello Rug".

Never make fun of people who make a mistake. Most don't even realize it. This patient got part of what I said but not completely. I sure wasn't going to try to correct her, I just smiled and hugged her and said, "Yeah that's me". She was happy and I was happy.

By the way she left the Psych Unit and went on to lead a successful life. Learn to roll with the flow and if someone you meet calls you the wrong name, just laugh and say, 'That's me'.

THROWING THE CAT DOWN

A church member asked that I come by her house to see her. She and her husband, a doctor, had a house in the foothills. It also had a place like on a ship where you could climb up to look out across the mountains. She was a photographer and when I drove up she said, "Go on in and I'll be down in a while, I'm waiting on my shot of the hills".

I went in and sat in the den to wait. Now she had fifteen cats. Each cat had its own color coordinated bed and the house was spotless. As I sat there, in walks an old tomcat. He walks up to me and hops up on my lap, because we're the only two in the room. I picked him up and threw him down from my lap. Well, he hops up again and I threw him down a little harder. Did I mention that I don't like cats? Well here he comes again and back on my lap.

Just as I was going to teach him to fly again, Beth walks down the stairs. She freezes and says, "How did you get him in your lap? He won't let me or Doc touch him. He tries to bite us".

Now, I got this cat that will attack on my lap. I freeze in the chair. Then the cat began digging his claws in my legs looking up at me. Beth says, "I would get him but he will bite me". She figured he was happy so we can talk for a while. After what seemed like eternity it was time to go. I rose up slowly and he hopped down and I headed home.

When I was able to see my legs it was like someone took pins and stuck them all over my legs. I guess I was lucky that he didn't attach me.

I wrote earlier that I don't like cats and this was one that I really grew to dislike. It was almost as if he was trying to get even with me for throwing him down. Well, he did. He put more punctures in me than I could count. Remember you can dislike an animal, just don't try and hurt it. Who knows if it might try and get even?

MORE PAIN

I had this elderly couple in the church I served. They were like peas in a pod. When you saw one you saw the other. Mr. Olin was a quiet man while the Mrs. Ollie never stopped talking. It was always an interesting visit because he and I would just shake our heads and she would talk.

He had to go to the hospital to have kidney surgery. I sat and listened to her while he was in surgery. You know you can get tired of just listening to someone who never stops talking. The surgery was successful.

The next day in the afternoon I went to the hospital to see him. When I arrived his wife was there and she started talking. He was on his back moaning from the pain. She said, "Preacher, they cut him from the front to the back around his side". I told her, "Yes, I knew they did".

"Preacher, it's a big cut, let me show you," she said going to the bed. "Honey, the preacher wants to see your scar," she told him. I said, "No, I am fine just let him rest". She then pulled the sheet back and grabbed him and turned him over. He is crying with pain as she moves him. She then takes the corner of the bandage and pulls it up.

"See preacher it's a big scar," she explained looking at me. Now he is in so much pain she says, "I believed he was more comfortable on his back". Speaking as she turned him over. He is crying, "Oh, Oh, Oh!" She responds, "Now honey the preacher wanted to see where they cut you, so go back to sleep." I often wondered how much he really enjoyed my visit. Sometimes I felt I became the pain man and not the peace man.

Always remember when a loved one is in the hospital it's not show and tell. The only sense of control they have is their bed. The staff controls everything else. That's why you never walk in a patient's room and just sit down on their bed. That's their space. Treat them like you want to be treated if you were in the bed. The last thing they need is more pain.

TWO CATS I LIKED

I don't like cats except two that I know of. Cats are so temperamental. You can pet one today and the next day it will scratch you.

Yet, I said I liked two cats, and the first one was a female that came to our farm. She had a tail that had been cut off leaving a stub of about five inches. The first thing she did was whip all the dogs including hunting dogs in the yard. When we fed the dogs in a trough she would walk up and they would duck their tails and step back.

I remember one time I heard one of the dogs crying and went to see what was going on. This cat had hooked her claws in his lip and was sitting there holding him. I made her let him go. I really liked this cat.

The second cat was owned by my Uncle Charlie. Now this cat would walk out into the open lawn and lay down. If a mocking bird or blue jay saw him they would begin diving at him. Closer and closer they would come and he would ignore them, twitching his tail slowly as they dove at him. Then all of a sudden as the bird came in he would spring into action and catch the bird in midair. Now that was something to watch that cat. I liked him too.

These were my two favorite cats, my only favorite cats. Each had a characteristic that I liked. One was brave and faced the dangers around her. The other had skills that amazed me and how he would catch a bird. They used these characterizes to survive. Friends, use your skills God gave you and face life head on. If you do you will remind me of the two cats I liked.

RIDING A PINE TREE DOWN

When I was growing up we didn't have many things to play with. We had to come up with creative ways to play. We could go to the creek, climb trees, or shoot a bow and arrow brought from the mountains. Cowboys and Indians were one of our favorite games.

We always looked for new excitement and such was an idea that came to us while sitting in a tree. The pine tree would grow small in diameter and tall. So why not climb up one then swing out holding the tree and it would gradually lower you to the ground. I don't know who was best but probably my brother. He would always have him test new ideas. He really did not have any choice when we told him.

Jimmy begins his climb and he is up fifteen or twenty feet and we said, "Grab the top of the tree and swing out". He did and it worked perfectly. I said I was next and began climbing the tree all the way to the top. Grabbing hold I was ready to swing out. Now I weighed more than my brother which I didn't think about. None of us had studied physics but we saw the success of the first try, so what could go wrong.

I gave a Tarzan yell and swung out and the top snapped sending me to the ground with the top of tree on me. It knocked the breath out of me and we all decided it was a bad tree. My cousin, Joe, went next and his was perfect. I retired for a while until my courage came back.

Yes, we all hit the ground from time to time but a successful ride down kept us riding the trees down. By the way my Dad asked me how the tops got broke out of the pines. I told him and I could tell by his response tree riding days were over.

Friends, you are lucky that you have things to play with, but be careful. You can get hurt on anything. I hope you have the good sense not to jump out of a tree at fifteen feet in the air. But you will do some crazy things as well. Use the brain God gave you to think about it first. What you do can be just a crazy as riding a pine tree down.

WADING THE CREEK WITH DAD

One of the highlights of summer was wading in the creek fishing with Dad. It occurred on one of those hot summer days when we would use Catawba worms for bait. The creek was a cold water stream and it felt good on a hot summer day.

We would step into the creek and it would be about knee deep. We fished the deeper areas ahead of us. As we fished and moved down the creek we would always encounter a snake.

There were cottonmouth moccasins along the way, some on logs, on the bank or just swimming the creek. The ones swimming were the ones you had to watch. Dad would see one coming toward us and he would say, "Just stand still and he will go by". The ones that were coming too close he would take the end of the cane and move them away. This is where I learned not to be afraid of snakes. Dad would never hurt one even though they were so poisonous. "Leave it alone and it will leave you alone," he would always say.

I have caught a chicken snake with my bare hands that were eating the chicken's eggs. Now, I killed him because he would be back if I had let him go. But never kill any animal without a good reason. Most will leave you alone if you leave them alone. Be respectful of God's creatures as my Dad did wading the creek with me.

MOTHER LATE FOR WEDDING

The wedding was scheduled to start at 5pm on Saturday. At the rehearsal the night before the bride's Mom was cautioned not to be late. She had a bad happen of being late.

The organist started playing at 4:30 pm as the guest arrived. At ten till the start time, the director came and informed me, "The bride's mom is not here." I said, "Let me know if she doesn't arrive in 5 minutes". She came back and told me she hadn't arrived yet.

I walked out to the organist and said, "The mother of the bride is not here so keep playing and I'll keep you posted". Around 5:15 pm I visited the organist again who at this time had played all the music he had brought. I then informed the guest that we are waiting on the bride's mother who is always late and we would start when she arrives. Eventually, at 6:45 pm she comes in and says, "Well I guess we can start now".

I told her not to hurry that I had already informed the guests why we hadn't started on time. She said, "I know you didn't". I said, "Yes, I told them we were waiting on the bride's mother who is always late". She turned and wheeled out of my office. You know she never spoke to me the rest of the night. By the way, the bride and groom were tickled that someone confronted her.

Always be on time for an occasion. If you can't make it let someone know. You know I believe on being on time in fact I'm always early. It says a lot about you if you are always late. This lady I believe would be late for her own funeral. Allow for time to get where you're going and don't wait till the last minute. You can relieve a lot of stress by starting fifteen minutes earlier. Don't be like the mother late for her daughter's wedding.

A TOILET RUNS AWAY

*I*t was my first appointment as a minister at this small town church. Once a month one of the activities was for the minister to accompany a Sunday School group of older adults on an outing. This would involve a supper somewhere. They had chosen a fish house and the date was set. We would have to drive cars because the church had no van or bus.

Now one of the ladies was just a negative cranky individual and a member said she can ride with the preacher. It was a horrible ride for me because I heard what was wrong with each person in the church. We finally arrived and proceeded to find our table which Ms. Ruby, bless my heart, decided to sit by me. She talked of how bad the service was; the food wasn't prepared right and how bad the baby was at the next table.

Ms. Ruby had to go to the bathroom and it was behind our table in the restaurant and had just one seat in each bathroom. She is complaining as she heads for the bathroom and her harsh last words before entering were, "This place is horrible". She shuts the door and quietness falls on our corner.

All of a sudden we hear a scream and some of the ladies exclaim, "Preacher, see if she is all right!" I remarked, "Don't you think one of you ladies ought to go?" "No, you can handle the situation," they added. I got up and went to the door. I knocked and said, "Ms. Ruby, are you okay?" She shouted back, "Get in here and help me!"

I took a deep breath and opened the door. Now what had happened was that this commode had fallen through the floor and she was at floor level. She had now entered the cussing mode of her language and was telling me she was going to sue.

I got some of the ladies in there to help me and we got her back to the table. She continued to fuss and the rest of the supper was ruined. The owner at the restaurant was as nice as he could be. He didn't know the floor had weakened. She didn't sue but she never put in a good word for them the rest of her life. Who knows she may be still complaining.

My dear friends, accidents happen in this life. It's nobody's fault they happened. But when it happens to someone with a bad attitude it makes it worst. Nothing would please Ms. Ruby at that moment or any moment beyond.

There are people in this world wired that way. I have met several. One clue, 'Avoid at all cost'. Just make sure you don't become like that, because the toilet may run away from you.

MY FIRST BLACK FUNERAL

I met Wash when I became a minister at this country church. He was born in Georgia and brought back to South Carolina by a Country doctor that attended the church I served years ago. Wash was on the streets down in Georgia and Doc brought him home to live with him. He raised him as a member of his family of four kids. As Wash grew older Doc built him a house out back. Wash got his name because he would wash up the utensils Doc would use during the day with patients.

Now Wash was up in age now but was still taken care of by the kids. Doc and his wife had already died. I treated him like any other member even though he went to the Baptist church. If he got sick I would visit him at home or hospital. Wash was a good man and I loved to sit and talk with him.

One day I got the call that Wash had died. I knew I would attend his funeral, because of my love for him and Doc's children.

I arrived at the church early to make sure I got a seat. Taking a bulletin I went in and saw Fran, one of Doc's daughters. I went and sat with her and told her I was so sorry and how hard this must be for the family. She agreed. When a lull in the conversation occurred, I looked at the bulletin and saw that I was to give the eulogy about Wash.

Turning to Fran I asked, "Am I to do the eulogy?" She said, "Yes, didn't Kat call you?" Responding I said "No". "What are you going to do?" she asked. "I guess I'm going to do a funeral", I responded.

I went to find the pastor of the church. He was excited for me to be there and that he looked forward to my words of comfort. Shaking my head I did not tell him I didn't have the words right then.

It was time so we went out as the choir was coming in. They would take one step then rock from side to side singing as they came down the aisle. Not realizing it I had begun to rock side to side with the choir. I was getting into the music. It took a while for them to get up front. When they got to the organ the individual playing the organ shouted a number and they shifted from low to high.

Now I was really into the music, the clapping of my hands and shifting my weight from foot to foot. What I was going to say was far from my mind, and I was feeling fine. We finally got seated. The host pastor was up first then a song and then I was up. It seemed that time was in high gear because it was time for me to get up.

Walking up to the pulpit I looked out across the congregation and said, "God loves us all". They responded, "Alright, Preach it Brother". I remarked, "God don't care if we are white or black, He loves us". Congregation then shouted, "Alright Brother, Preach it, Help Him Jesus". I continued one liners the rest of the way and more and more answers from the congregation. This experience would help me at the next appointment when I paired with the black church to exchange pulpits and other happenings together. But this funeral prepared me and was one of the greatest experiences in my life.

I have learned to trust God in situations like this. He has never let me down and that's why I love Him so. Develop a personal relationship with Him and He will never let you down.

KATHRYN SPEAKS COWAH

I took a team of twelve to the Cowah Indian Reservation for a mission trip. We were to work on the church they were building. It was a successful trip with a lot accomplished.

We arrived back at home and the following Sunday I had each of the team members to share their experience and how God used them. Before the service I met with Kathryn. She was one of those quiet serious team members. I asked her to do something with me during the service. The plan was for her to go up to the mike and address the crowd in the Cowah language. I would explain what was going to happen with me translating the language.

Kathryn steps up and says, "Na ha na ha ha". I step up and say, "Good morning". Stepping back Kathryn steps up and said, "Wa now com ya ha". I stepped up and answered, "It's good to be with you this morning". She steps up again and loses it which opened the door for the church to laugh.

Nobody expected Kathryn to do something like this. This was the beginning of her losing up. She later became a minister in the Methodist Church. I was so proud of her and love her to pieces.

There is nothing wrong with having fun in the church. So many in the church have this serious look and say to you, 'I've got the joy of the Lord in my heart'. Boy it makes you say 'I want that'.

Remember there is not one shred of evidence to prove life is serious, we make it serious. Learn to laugh and have fun because God likes that. I saw Kathryn a few weeks ago and I shared the story and we both laughed. It was so good to see her laugh, really laugh.

THANKSGIVING AT AUNT MAUDES

A highlight of the year was having Thanksgiving at Aunt Maude's house. It was a time when all my uncles, aunts and cousins were all together. We would all arrive early. The cousins and I would play football in the front yard. Now, this was special for us to play for we had an audience of family on the porch.

When it was time for dinner the food was unbelievable to say the least. The dinner consisted of turkey, ham, rice, dressing, macaroni and cheese, green beans and a host of other vegetables and salads. The deserts were of every variety such as cakes, pies, cookies and of course banana pudding which I dearly loved.

After lunch we were too full to do anything so we would sit and listen to my uncles tell stories. My uncles Jim, Charlie, Ed and Smick would tell stories of their growing up. Boy, they could make you laugh. The sharing of stories helped me in the ministry with sermons. I just told a story. I still remember a lot of those times with them and the stories that were told.

Also, this was the time when each person drew a name for a Christmas gift. Everybody's name was placed in a hat and each person drew a name. That was the person's gift we would bring to our Christmas dinner.

Then about mid-afternoon it was time for the annual rabbit hunt for everyone who was old enough. I will talk about a specific one hunt in another story.

Thanksgiving was a time of food, fellowship, fun, and family. During this time families were together. Very few families gather like this anymore. Most families are like a group of quail when flushed, they fly in all different directions. Its hard today to get families together and I miss it in my own family. Oh, would I like to have a place like Aunt Maude's home again so we all could gather. Now that would be great!

BLEEDING TO DEATH

I had by-pass surgery and had come home after the hospital stay. Having had six by-passes I came home to take it easy. The last thing I wanted was to fall and bust myself open.

My wife had to go to check on her Dad which was admitted to the hospital in ICU, so she left me home alone. I assured her I would be fine. Though she would be over an hour away I had the neighbors. Everything would be fine.

It was late evening and I decided I would go to the mailbox to get the newspaper. Putting on my slippers I started out. I had to go down three steps to the sidewalk and then about fifty feet to the box. Starting down the steps my shoe slipped and I fell over onto my back on wet sidewalk. Feeling the wet shirt I thought that I was bleeding. The fall had busted me open and I would die right here. Laying on the ground dying I looked for my neighbors but no one was home. I was going to die right there in the yard.

As the time went by my death didn't come and I decided to try and get up. Rolling to my knees I got up and slowly made my way into the house. Entering into the light, I could see there was no blood and I felt better.

Keeping quiet I told no one but when I went to the doctor I asked him about falling. Dr. Smith commented, "Don't worry I wired you up real good".

Dear friends, it's amazing what can scare you in this life. This incident really scared me. I should have listened to the doctor, the staff and my wife, but I didn't. So look what happened.

You always need to listen in all situations of life no matter how small. As a minister I have seen a lot of stupid things by people that wind up hurting themselves. Be wise and listen and you won't think you are bleeding to death.

CATCHING A GOOSE

Growing up on the farm we were close to being self-sufficient. We raised vegetables and animals for food. We ground corn at a local mill for grits and meal. We raised chickens for eggs and meat. Dad would also raise turkeys, ducks, and geese. Turkeys and the geese were harvested at Thanksgiving and Christmas.

Now I was the oldest son, so Dad had me to catch the turkey and goose. Have you ever caught a big male turkey? It's an experience. Dad and I would go into the pen and he would say, "Son, catch that big turkey". I've caught chickens but a turkey is totally different. Like a fox I moved into position and I jumped out and caught him by the legs. He beat me with those big wings and I wanted to let go of him. Dad kept yelling, "Hold him son, hold him!" I closed my eyes and held on until Dad came to help me. Now a turkey is bad news, but a goose is worst.

When I caught my first goose they not only beat you with their wings but they also pinch you with that bill. They can really pinch you with that beak. I had to make several catches of that goose because of the biting and beating of the wings. After a while I finally got him. Thank the Lord Dad didn't get another goose after that episode. Dad laughed and enjoyed my first and last goose catching.

There are some hard things in life we have to do. When you get into some situations you will want to quit because it beats you down. It can be with a friend, school, a job, marriage, family or child. I would say to you to pray for guidance. Yes, it's like catching a goose but hang in there for help will arrive.

SANDRA SLAPPED ME

When I was young, we had to ride the school bus to school. It was a one hour ride. Now for a young boy an hour is a long time to entertain yourself. Somebody was going to get aggravated.

My two cousins, Sandra and Libby were also some of the first to get on the bus like me, my brother and other cousins. We sat behind them on the bus. So who did I have to aggravate except the two of them. Sandra was the best target for she had pigtails. You don't need brain power to figure out what to do here. Just pull the pigtails when she wasn't looking.

Now I must confess I pulled them several times but this morning I was quiet. Yet, one of the other boys behind me wanted to get involved, so he reached up over the seat and 'Yanked the pigtails'.

Now I was sitting there innocent as a lamb and Sandra turned around and slaps the tar out of me. I saw stars. She then exclaimed to me, "Don't pull my hair anymore"! I tried to let her know it wasn't me but it fell on deaf ears. She is the only person who has ever slapped my face.

Friends, it's hard to plead your case when you were guilty before. I never pulled her hair after that; it was a wakeup call for me. Did I deserve that slap 'No', but for the other times 'Yes'. Always be careful aggravating a person or animal. Each will reach a point when you will get scratched or bit or even get slapped.

GOD GIVES A PARKING PLACE

Your knees can take you where your feet cannot.

I have visited the hospital numerous times in my forty four years as a minister. Parking has always been a problem, but I learned to ask God for a parking place.

Now this has amazed me when I would drive up in a full parking lot and have a car begin to back out of their space. I would thank God and park. This has happened hundreds of times over the years.

In life I have learned to ask God for the little things in life. Many times when I would ask for the little things, they didn't grow into big things. Take all things to God in prayer and He will help.

Yet to most people will not ask for help from God until they paint themselves into a corner. By then the situation has grown from bad to worst. God is standing by to help, but people think they are smarter than He is, so they try to handle the problem.

The scripture says God is concerned about the little sparrow so I know He is concerned to help me with a parking place when I need it.

'God is Good, All the Time, God is Good'

SOMETHING IS COMING DOWN THE PIPE

One summer I worked with my cousin installing time clocks. This required a lot of wires coming from different locations in the building. Wire would have to run to heating or cooling units or other items. This required a lot of conduit (metal pipe to run the wires) in the system. The conduit ranged in size from half inch to two inches in diameter.

We had spent a day running the pipe and planned to pull the wires in it the next day. The following morning we took a fish tape and forced it into the conduit. A fish tape is a long piece of metal wire that we ran into the pipe to attach the wires so that we could pull them through it. Pete, my cousin, was upstairs pushing the tape down to me through the conduit. "You hear anything?" Pete asked. "Yes, something is coming down the pipe".

Holding my ear to the pipe as the tape drew closer I stood by to grab the tape. I was waiting patiently for the tape to come through pipe, when suddenly out jumps a rat from inside the pipe onto my shoulder. I broke into my dance routine to get him off me. Yes, something was coming down the pipe, a rat.

I used this phrase when we had prayer time in the church. I would always remind them that there is always something coming down the pipe of life. So get ready for whatever it make be.

Pray for a faith to be able to stand firm in whatever it is. Could be sickness, sudden death of a friend or family member, a financial surprise and on and on it comes. It may be small or it could be large. So get ready for there is always something coming down that pipe.

MY DAD

My Dad was one of those men who didn't show his emotions. I never heard my Dad say to me, 'I love you'. He was a good man and a good provider. He didn't talk much and when he did people would listen. He was a strict Dad that when he told you something to do, don't try and negotiate a better deal. What he said we did.

I learned a lot from Dad. I learned to hunt, garden, cook and be a man of your word. He served in World War II under General Patton and came home unhurt. I learned to be a man under my Dad.

Dad loved mom and my brother but it was hard for him to show it. Mom always hugged us but that wasn't Dad, yet we knew he loved us. It would have been good to hear it though.

My Dad died suddenly with complications from a kidney stone. He threw a blood clot and it went to his heart and he died. My son and I had visited him hours before this happened.

I came down to take care of the animals for him. Dad and Brandon, my son, talked of going fishing. It was a fun time between the two of them. It came time to go and I asked Dad, "May I have prayer with you?" He said, "Yes, I would like that". Now I have a habit with church members that after I pray I lightly grab their toe and say, "I love you". Out of habit I did that to Dad and he looked at me and he said, "I love you too". That was the first time I remember my Dad saying those words, not knowing those were going to be the last words he said to me on this side of heaven. I had received a great blessing from him. Three hours later he would be dead. Oh the timing of God is so awesome.

Friends and families let each other know that they are loved. Tell them that you love and appreciate them. I wouldn't trade anything for those words from Dad. Just four little words 'I love you, too'. Hope each of you hold a special place in your heart of family and friends.

ALABAMA TRIP

*T*he Cattleman's Association of which I'm a member, put together a trip to Alabama. We were to visit various sights along the way and then ended up with a trip to Teddy Gentry's farm. Teddy is the bass player for the group, 'Alabama'.

We arrived in Fort Payne, Alabama to spend the night before going to the farm the next morning. My roommate was Tommy, a church member. Now on this trip we had three of my crazy friends. Alton, Stanley, and Glenn were always doing something crazy. Before we went to bed they came by to let Tommy and I know that we would meet for breakfast. There was a restaurant down the street where we would meet at eight o'clock.

The next morning when we got up and headed down it was raining cats and dogs. Tommy and I decided we would just eat breakfast at the motel and not go out into the rain.

Meanwhile down at the restaurant my three friends had told everyone that we would be arriving soon. Also, they told them that we had just come out of the closet and wanted the people to support us because we were shy. Now the restaurant was filled with customers and they were waiting on us. Thank God for rain and we missed it.

Readers, crazy friends make life interesting. These guys would do anything for me and they are good friends. Yet, they are a little crazy at times. Life is pretty dull if all you have are straight level people, serious all the time. I am about a half bubble off plumb myself. I can take it but I can dish it out. I love Alton, Stanley, and Glenn and would do anything for them. They are my good friends. Let me also say Tommy is right there with them. Life is interesting when God provides friends like this. Each of you should have a variety of friends and life will be interesting and fun. As much fun as the trip I took with my friends to Alabama.

JUST US

*T*here's a restaurant in Cayce, a part of Columbia, South Carolina called 'Just Us'. If you are in the area I encourage you to stop by. The food is great, good portions, and reasonable prices. The owner (Mark) is friendly, loveable and cute. The staff is unbelievable and work like a well-oiled machine.

The customers know each other and it is just a great fellowship with family every time we go. By the way, I have an adopted son, (Dee) who works there, but he looks like his mother. My wife and I eat there three or four times a week.

My favorite meal is breakfast and I order the same thing each time. I sung my order on one occasion and now I have to sing to the waitresses on each occasion. When I order this is what I sing:

Two eggs smashed
With some grits
Onion sausage
With a swipe of mustard on it
Don't want no jelly
It goes to my belly
Just some dry wheat toast
Thank you dear you're the most!

It's just a fun place that you will leave feeling good. These are rare places indeed and it's for us, 'Just Us'. Find you a fun place to mingle with people. Learn to laugh with them not at them. Get to know the staff and be kind and respective of them. . This is my laughing place to be myself. God has blessed this place and I pray for them every night that business will be good. They in turn bless me. But what would you expect when it's 'Just Us'.

MISSING FINGERS

G rowing up I was close to my family, Uncle Ed and Uncle Charlie. I would help them with projects on their farm and learned a lot from both. Some of these projects were small and others were large such as working on big equipment.

It was a cold fall day and Uncle Ed was checking the tractor for antifreeze. It was getting late as he looked at the water pump and said, "I don't think that belt is turning". Sticking his finger in against the pulley it caught his pointing finger, cutting it off at the first knuckle.

When Uncle Charlie found out that his brother had cut his finger off he remarked, "That was the stupidest thing for a grown man to do, just stupid". He gave Uncle Ed a fit about the cutting off of his finger.

A month or two later I was helping Uncle Charlie work on the combine. There is an inspection plate that you remove to see if the belt is turning. Again it is getting dark with little light to see and the round wheel that houses the clutch can't be seen. Uncle Charlie had this dim flash light trying to see if it was turning. "I don't think it's turning son," He hollered to me. Taking his pointer finger he sticks it in to see if it was turning. Whan! Off goes the end of his finger. Uncle Ed had a field day, when he found out that Uncle Charlie had done the same stupid thing too, by checking to see if the belt was turning with his pointer finger.

Friends, someone outside our family would think the family had a genetic defect missing the pointer finger. No, it was just stupidity. Now, don't get on them too much. I don't, for I have done stupid things in the past. News flash, people will do some stupid things in their life, if not already. Think before you do something or you may lose a finger too.

NASCAR IN GEORGETOWN

*K*eith, Chet, Rachael (my daughter) and I flew to the coast to fish on a Charter boat. We flew down with Keith to the Georgetown Airport. They had an old car that they kept at the airport to get to where we were staying. We would be arriving at the peak of the five o'clock traffic in Georgetown, South Carolina.

It was a hot summer day and we were traveling in stop and go traffic. We knew the battery was weak and so there wouldn't be any air-condition, radio or lights as we traveled. To enhance the situation it started raining but no wipers except every now and then they would work.

As we approached the intersection the light turns red. While waiting for the light to turn, the car shuts off, and then the light turns green. Keith and I jump out with a power pack to boost the battery. I open the hood and Keith puts the clamps on. "Try it", I said to Chet and the engine fires up. Then off comes the clamps and down comes the hood and we are off again. We did this in a record time. Might I say that Keith, an attorney, had just left work, so he was dressed to the max. Not only were we quick but we looked good too.

Friends, it is great when everyone pulls together as a team in a bad situation. Keith and I had never practiced this before but we just knew what to do. It's always great when people work together as in churches because things get accomplished.

Life is better when couples work together and when children work with their Mom and Dad. The workplace runs smoother when everyone is on the same page. Remember one person can mess up the plan if they are not a team player. Learn to be a team player in life and if that happens things will come together like NASCAR in Georgetown.

SOGGY BOTTOM DEBUE

The youth were having a talent show and were looking for participants. I talked with a friend of mine, Tommy, about getting a group together to be the Soggy Bottom Boys and sing the song from the movie 'O Brother Where Art Thou'. As we talked it over the following individuals were elected to be a part of the group: Luther, Shag, Tommy, Dennis and myself.

I got them all to agree to do it for the youth. We would pantomime the song 'Of Constant Sorrow'. When we practiced Tommy and Luther found out they had to dance after we watched the movie. They would also lip-synch a few words. They practiced their moves as the time drew near. Shag and Dennis were the musicians and I was the lead singer.

The night of the performance came and we were back stage, Tommy and Luther were still working on their dance moves. Tommy finally tells Luther to sit down because he was making him nervous. Luther comes over to me and says, "I'm glad you are a good man because if you were a bad man no telling what you would have us do". He and Tommy kept saying, "How did you talk us into this".

The curtain is pulled back and we go on. The music begins and I get ready to sing, then Tommy and Luther began to dance. When we finish they were wet with sweat. The crowd loved it and had a great time.

Remember it is good to be a kid again and have some fun. Here we are grown men doing something crazy for the youth. Never let the kid in you die, keep them alive. Rest assured the kid in me is big time alive. Learn to enjoy life. By the way Tommy volunteered to sing with a group in church recently. The Soggy Bottom Boys helped him to dance and led him to sing. God is Good!

JUMPING IN A COLD BED

When I grew up we only had fireplaces in the home for heat in the winter. We had a stove in the kitchen to cook on and getting up wood was a daily chore for us.

My Dad would build a fire in the fireplace to warm the room. A fireplace is a poor source of heat because most of the heat goes up the chimney. So at bed time we would pull the covers back and stand as close as we could to the fire to warm up.

Just before blistering ourselves, we would run and jump in that cold bed. There were approximately six to eight inches of cover on us, so when we got warm, sleep came easy.

The next morning we would have to get up and jump out of bed into a cold room which was no fun. We would run to the living room by the fire that Dad had brought to life after burning slow all night. Jimmy (my brother) and I would get ready for school by the warm fire.

Granny would be cooking breakfast on that wooden stove. I remember that just as cold as it was in the winter, it was just as hot in the summer. By the way, bathing was in a tin tub by the fire.

Friends, we had no central air or heat. Also, we didn't have a bathroom either. Yet, there was plenty to eat and a Mom and Dad that loved us.

They provided for us the best they could which also taught us to be survivalist and to appreciate what we had. Looking back I never remember us being poor, though some people would say we were. It was just a way of life.

Always be thankful for what you have and be appreciative of all things big and small. These are gifts from God. Make sure you thank those who raised you. I know I thanked God for my parents when I jumped in that cold bed for warmth was coming.

MY FEAR OF A CATERPILLAR

*T*here are many things I am not afraid of; snakes, rats, mice, spiders and etc., they don't shake me. Some people have a phobia of these things. Not even walking in the woods at night ever frightened me, I was comfortable. There is one thing, however, that I am deathly afraid of, caterpillars.

If you throw one of those on me I will hurt you. Even when the kids were small they would bring one of those creepy things in to show me. I would threaten them and say, "Get that thing away from me!" I do believe if someone threw a handful of them on me, my life would be over. A heart attack would surely take me out.

I never got use to those things after all these years and I don't see that changing. Maybe I can touch one in heaven, but I don't look forward to it.

Friends, everybody has fears. There are lots of fears in this world. There is the fear of animals, heights or places, but there are other fears.

I have found that people have three basic fears. The fear of faces, the fear of failure, and the fear of the future, are all a part of life.

The fear of faces involves what people think of me, do they like me? This fear is so great in teenagers. Just remember that everybody will not like you. It would be bad if certain people did like you.

The second is the fear of failure, failing in life. Did I let people down? I can't fail in life, but you will. Just pack up the pieces and move on. We all fail every day.

Lastly is the fear of the future. How will my health be? Will I have enough finances? What will my children become? As a minister I have found that most people have these fears in life.

So what can you do about these fears? Ask God to help you with your fears. Let me quickly add that he is still working with me on those darn caterpillars.

A COW WILL GET FAT ON GRASS

A close friend of mine, Billy, and I both had heart surgery and attended cardiac rehab together. Billy was a member at the church I served. We would ride together to exercise.

On Fridays we would have to meet with the dietitian about our diet. She would tell us what to avoid and what to eat. Salads were an important part of the menu. We would listen and then when she finished some of the individuals in the exercise room would ask, "Where are ya'll going for lunch?" I would answer, "Antley's BBQ, they have a buffet". "I know you're not!" one of the other patients would exclaim. "Oh, yes," Billy would laughingly reply.

They couldn't believe we were actually going to eat Bar B Que, but we were. Some in the class would remind us what the dieticiton had said about salads. I reminded them, "That even a cow will get fat on grass". That's hard to argue. We left and headed to Antley's Bar B Que with fried chicken.

Readers, we grew up on pork, beef, chicken and wild game. My family is a group of long living individuals. By the way, if we ate only what they want us to eat there would be few items to eat. The ones they recommend wouldn't have much taste to them either. I would rather die fat and happy instead of thin and miserable. I think the key word is moderation. Eat a little of everything, not just salads for cows get fat on grass.

SITTING ON MY BACK PORCH

$\mathcal{M}$y back porch faces Columbia and the lights of the city are visible. Planes can be seen circling over my farm to line up for landing at the airport. I watch the flashing lights until the plane descends below the tree line. A distant train can be heard hauling supplies to the chemical plant.

A whippoorwill is calling for his mate across the field. An owl is hooting as he gets ready to begin his night hunt and the coyotes are singing as they too get ready for their night hunt. Lighting bugs dot the horizon with light as thousands of the stars fill the sky. Bats are flying around the night lights as they feed on bugs.

In the distance the moon is rising from behind the trees giving light to the night. As it clears the trees the silhouette of my cows can be seen in the pasture. The night is so alive as I sit here. This is my place to relax and spend time with God. It's a time when we can just talk for this is my special plaice.

Readers, everyone needs a place they can just relax and a place that promotes peace and rest. We need to just stop sometimes in life from the fast pace. My porch is that place for me and I'm so glad that God takes time to sit with me on my back porch.

EATING BAD CHITLINS

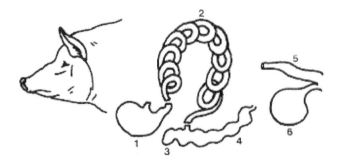

I have always loved chitlins. Started eating them at a young age and know how they are supposed to taste. You might say it's an acquired taste.

At my first appointment, I had the opportunity to eat some chitlins. A church member asked if I liked them and I said, "Yes". He was going to kill a hog on Monday and he would save some chitlins for me. The large intestines of a hog are what the chitlins are made of and he was going to cook them Friday night. I was excited for this special occasion.

Friday night comes and it's a cold rainy night. I enter the house and I am hit with this smell. Trying to ignore it, Mr. Jack gets ready to serve us. He had boiled them and I had always eaten them fried. They looked like little flowers. He then took the water he had boiled them in and added grits. Mr. Jack dipped a large bowl of grits and added three of those chitlins. The smell was tuff and when I tasted one it just wasn't right. I knew there was no way I could eat them as they had been prepared.

"Do you have any ketchup and mustard?" I asked. He got some for me and I covered everything masking some of the taste. One plate and bowl was enough. The next day they were still with me.

Friends, never agree to eat something unless you know the cook and what it is. If I had known before how they were being prepared, I would have been busy Friday. Yet, I went and was trapped. Thank God for mustard and ketchup for it helped some.

In the ministry I've had to eat a lot of things I didn't like, but this was the worst. So pay attention to what you eat and how it is prepared. Don't be afraid to try new things but if it smells bad don't eat it.

HERE COMES AN EMU

I had just moved to my next appointment and was sitting at my desk looking out of the window. All of a sudden a white horse runs by and disappears down the dirt road by the parsonage.

Few days later sitting at my desk another animal walks by my window and this time it was an emu. Then it goes down the same dirt road. I get in the truck with my wife and mother-in-law to see if we could find the emu down the dirt road.

We came to a church member's farm and Duwayne was out by the chicken houses where they raise chickens. Now let me tell you, this was the first time to meet some members of my new church. We drove up and got out. Duwayne, his wife Linda and brother-in-law (Connie) are standing there. We speak and then I tell him about the emu. "He walked right by my window and came this way," I said. "Emu, do say don't see many of those around here in fact, I've never seen one over here," Duwayne said. "Are you sure it was an emu?" He added. "Yes, I've seen them before," I replied. "How big was he?" asked Duwayne. Now I can tell if someone believes me or not and I could tell he didn't. Wonder what they thought of their new minister.

I tried again by repeating, "He came down the road". Again Duwayne answered, "Do say". About this time I looked up and what do I see but the emu coming down the driveway. "There he is," I shouted and feeling so relieved. "It sure is an emu," Duwayne said. Thank God he sent that emu to help me out that day.

Readers, have you ever been talking to someone and you know they don't believe you? They're looking at you but thinking I don't believe this. Oh, they try to be nice but you know your words are falling on deaf ears. No matter what you say it doesn't help but they are still so nice. Sometimes it's best to just walk away, because you can't convince them. So hang in there if you think an emu might come walking up.

HERE COMES THE BRIDE

*T*he couple wanted to have a cowboy wedding. Everyone would be dressed as a cowboy or cowgirl. I would look like I was right out of the old west with my long coat on.

The rehearsal and supper went well at the groom's Mon and Dad's house the night before the wedding. The couple was getting married at the groom's grandparent's old home place which was over the holler from where we had the rehearsal. The grandparent's house was at the bottom of a slopping field with terraces running through the land.

The bride would get ready at the groom's house and then get into a stagecoach to come across the field just at the right time to make her entrance. The coach was driven by 'Cowboy' (the drivers' nick name) pulled by two horses.

It was time for the wedding but Cowboy was running late. He arrived about ten minutes late and he hurriedly hitched the coach and horses. The wedding and guest were already waiting for the entrance of the bride. Everyone can see the bride enter the coach and the door shuts.

Cowboy hollows, "Hi" and here comes the bride. When the coach would hit one of those terraces the bride would disappear and then reappear until the next terrace. The coach, Cowboy and the bride came sliding into the yard. This was like an old western movie where the stagecoach out runs the outlaws.

She rises up and her vail was turned sideways. After she had found her land legs the wedding began. This wedding was unique and I was honored to officiate, but I will never forget Cowboy.

This was a fun wedding for me. I will never forget that coach coming across those terraces. I know the bride was sore the next day. Cowboy wanted to be on time so he tried his best. This was something he could have helped if he had left earlier. Readers, always try to be a little early to anything you attend especially if you're involved in the occasion. Usually when you have to hurry the odds are higher you will mess up, just as Cowboy did when he brought the bride to the wedding late.

GETTING PVC COUPLINGS

I had to have heart by-pass surgery which resulted in six by-passes. At the same time a friend of mine, Billy, also had to have by-pass surgery. It worked out that we did cardiac rehab at the same time in Orangeburg.

When I drove to Columbia to visit members in the different hospitals, I would watch the roadside for PVC pipe couplings that had fallen off a truck. These would be on the interstate roads around Columbia. I would make a note for Billy and myself so that we could come back that night to get them. I was renovating my Mom's house and I could use them.

Now, the timing had to be right with the traffic. We would pull on the shoulder of the road and wait for a clearing in the traffic, then dash across and get the PVC. Sometimes we would get three or four in a night. This was done late at night so we could go and get coffee and donuts afterwards.

Billy and I did this exercise while we were under our surgeons care. It was exercise to us, but I'm not sure what our doctors would have thought. Anyway we ended up with PVC couplings, all sizes and shapes. I used them all in my Mom's house in the renovation.

Friends, running across an interstate after heart surgery is not smart, yet we did it. Both of us are still alive today and I would be lying to you if I told you there were no close calls. Just between you and me there were.

Don't do as I did, listen to your doctor they know best. Don't be crazy like Billy and me running across the interstate to get a PVC coupling.

A MOUTHFUL OF TEETH

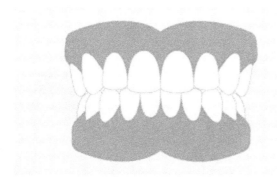

$\mathcal{M}$r. D owned a hardware store in a small town where I had been appointed by the Methodist Church to be their minister. On mornings when I didn't have any members having surgeries or in the hospitals, I would stop by and talk with him before breakfast. I would stop by his store three or four times a week just to talk. Mr. D was a good friend of mine.

One morning I dropped by and Mr. D looked different. All I could notice was his teeth. He had a mouth full, in fact more teeth than he needed. It affected his speech as he kept adjusting them. I didn't say anything because I was caught off guard. We talked for a while longer and then the phone rang.

It's his wife calling. Mr. D answers the phone and asks, "What's wrong?" I can't hear her words but he kept saying, "Yes… Yes…. Yes ma'am".

In a little while Mrs. D shows up and mad as a wet sitting hen. I'm standing by the paint display and she can't see me. I heard her say, "You took my teeth!" After some more choice words she sees me and apologizes for her comments. The two of them exchanged teeth and I wanted to laugh, but instead just stood there quiet.

I never encountered this again in my ministry. I think of Mr. D every time I see one of those dental commercials where they say, "We can lift and push out your teeth to give you that perfect smile."

Mr. D's smile was pushed out, up and everywhere. He certainly had an awesome grin with a lot of teeth. I did both of their funerals and loved them both very much. I remember them both fondly, especially the day Mr. D had that mouth full of teeth.

TWO DOGS IN THE WEDDING

*I*t was one of those mountain outdoor weddings. The place was beautiful. We met for the rehearsal the night before and it went without a hitch except they were going to use their dogs as the flower girl and ring bearer.

Now, I thought this is going to be interesting. Parents have a hard enough time with young kids and I didn't know what to expect with two dogs. I can imagine those dogs running all over the place, during the ceremony. Oh well, it's what the couple wanted so let it be. It's their wedding and not mine.

The next evening was the first time that I saw the dogs, they were running and hopping around. One was a pug which was the ring bearer and the small poodle was the flower girl. Thinking to myself, 'This is going to be wild.'

It was time to start and the best man, groom and I go out. Then the groomsmen, bride maids and maid of honor walk to their places. I took a deep breath because it was time for the dogs to enter. The little poodle comes out first with a basket of rose petals on her back. The poodle would be joined by the ring bearer, the pug, with the rings on a pillow on his back. Now that flower dog would take a few steps and stop and shake petals out of the basket that was on her back.

When she would stop the pug would stop to wait on her. Now they did this all the way down the aisle and then went and sat down by their owners. The poodle belonged to the bride and the pug to the groom. I had never seen anything like this before in my life. They did it better than most kids. I was amazed.

Friends, I had the outcome of this wedding figured wrong. I thought it was going to be a wreck with these two dogs. These animals were smart and well trained and they performed on cue. They were better behaved than a lot of children I have seen in my ministry.

A child has to be trained by loving parents so that they can perform in life. If you turn a young person loose in life with no limits that child is doomed. Remember there are laws in life and they will break you. Remember what you have learned and taught in life and you will be a success like those two dogs.

LOSING A FINGER

Things were going smooth for a weekday. I had recently got my driver's licenses and life was good. The phone rings and its Mrs. Lavinia, a neighbor. She tells me that she has cut her finger off and needs to be taken to the emergency room. Rucker's ambulance (1) springs into action.

Arriving at her home she was waiting to get in the car. Her hand has a wash cloth wrapped around and it was soaked in blood. Mrs. Lavinia gets in and off we go to the emergency room. I asked her if she cut the finger off and she responded, "I think so". She unwraps the hand and the finger falls on the floor under my feet on the driver's side.

"I lost my finger!" She cried out. "I'll get it," I said, "Everything will be ok." Now, have you ever had to find a finger on the floor while driving on the interstate highway? It's an eerie feeling trying to find it but I did. She put it back in place and wrapped it up again.

We arrived at the emergency room and go in. The nurse asks if it was completely cut off, and we both said, "Yes", but she had to look at it. Removing the wash cloth, the finger falls on the floor. Mrs. Lavinia tried to pick it up but she is missing one finger in the process. The other finger on her hand hits the loose finger on the floor and it scoots along on the floor. The other patients in the emergency room began to feel sicker after seeing her finger slide across the floor, so the nurse springs into action.

The nurse finally is able to grab it and picks up the finger. They take her back but can't save the finger. All I can say is that my day turned out interesting.

Friends, it's always good to help people in a time of need when they call. When someone calls for help it's not a time for a lot of questions, just be there for them. I left thinking her finger was somewhat intact. Boy was I wrong. It was hard for me to try and pick that finger up. Yet I did it. In situations like this adrenaline kicks in and we do what we have to do. Always, remember to whisper a prayer for help when driving on the interstate highway trying to find a finger.

I CAUGHT BILLY

I had just moved to this appointment and was getting to know the people. One of the members was an undercover deputy. I really hadn't got to meet him yet.

We had a problem with people meeting behind our gym at the church. There was always some car parked back there. One afternoon I noticed a car back of the gym so I called 911 and reported a suspicious activity behind our gym. When the deputy sheriff arrived I was there to meet him. I walked where I could see what was going on. There were other deputies located behind the church and they had someone in a car.

I had no idea who they had captured, but I was glad they were getting him off the street. About that time, one of the deputies asked the criminal, "what are you doing back here?' He answers holding up a little bag, "I am selling weed". Thinking to myself, they have got him. Now, to my surprise, they all left the scene even the criminal by himself in his own car. I later found out the criminal, Billy, was one of my church members and the undercover deputy. I had turned in one of my own church members. I met him at church later and we laughed about the episode. Billy and I still laugh about that today.

Always get the facts before you make your mind up on something. You see I put two and two together and got five. It's easy to come up with a story in your own mind. We had captured a drug dealer behind our church gym.

What we figured was true except he was a good guy. Billy no longer does this type of work after being shot in the line of duty. He had to retire. He is one of my best friends and I love him and his dear family to death and we still laugh about the time I caught Billy.

PREDICTING THE WEATHER

*E*very night I watch the local news and weather. The weather has become so sophisticated with all the technology. The maps and graphs are so awesome. Now we don't have the weathermen or weatherwomen, but we have meteorologists and one is the chief. They can tell us to the minute when rain will occur or the storm arrives. Even your telephone is plugged in to them and it will give you an alert. It has become so sophisticated.

When I grew up we didn't have a television to get the forecast. All we had was my grandfather and my dad. Granddaddy would put a plug of Brown Mule tobacco in his mouth, chew a moment then spit. He would then say, "Wind is from the south and listen to how clear the air is with the night sounds, it will rain tomorrow."

The next day it would rain. My granddaddy read the sounds of nature. I wish I had written some of them down. A ring around the moon, an abundance of nuts on trees, or the cry of a rain crow all gave meaning. Again, I wish I could remember all these signs of nature and their meanings.

Sometimes as I listen to the meteorologist my mind drifts back to that porch and granddaddy. I can see him cut a piece of Brown Mule chewing tobacco and began to chew. He would spit on the ground and look at the sky and say, "Wind is out of the south. He would continue by saying, "Listen to those crickets and that whippoorwill, the air is real clear, it is so clear tonight. Also, I heard a rain crow calling today, so it will rain tomorrow." My granddaddy was right on target predicting rain, for it did rain the next day.

I would encourage every meteorologist to take a drive into the country. Away from city lights, and get out and listen to the night sounds. Feel that south wind on your cheek and the clarity of the night creatures singing in the night. I think this experience would make a meteorologist better forecasters. By the way, don't forget your umbrella tomorrow.

Matthew Rucker

HAVE SOME SUGAR CANE

Every fall my Dad would make sugar care syrup. He would start by cutting the sugar cane and then store the stalks until they were ready to be squeezed. We had a mill that did the squeezing.

We started in the morning and had almost fifty five gallons of juice squeezed. It was during this time that a traveling salesman showed up. His car contained almost everything. Dad was busy and didn't have time for him.

The salesman saw the sugar cane and said that he remembered eating it when he was a kid. He asked if he could have some of the juice. I got a quart jar and filled it up for him to try. He was pleased and drank it down. He asked for a refill and I got another quart for him. Now, it's important to know that sugar cane juice is a powerful laxative when drinking a lot.

In a short while when he was showing Dad some other products he started shifting around. He asked if we had a bathroom. Dad said, "Yes, in the house to the left, my wife will show you."

He went in the house and was gone for a while. Finally, he came out, got to the bottom of the steps, turns around and headed inside again. Some time passes and here he comes out of the house, gets halfway down the steps and back in the house he went.

He finally came out and came back down to us and said, "I'm sorry but something has upset my stomach." He got ready to leave but before he left, he asked if he could take a jar of juice with him. "Oh, yes," I said and he left with the juice. No more salesmen to hinder our work. I did ask my Dad, "I wonder how far he got."

When you're trying to do work and someone is hindering your ability to get it done it's aggravating. In this case I offered him something to drink and remember he wanted more. I got rid of him and we completed our work and made the syrup. We couldn't get him to leave so when you have someone who is hindering you with their presence offer them some sugar cane juice.

DAD'S APPLE TREE GOES DOWN

My Dad raised cows on our farm where we grew up. One day Dad and I put up an electric fence to keep the cows in the pasture. Now, these electric fences have quite a kick especially if the ground is wet. We finished putting the fence up and plugged it in. Now, the fence was live.

We had a Herford bull, Bully, weighting about fifteen hundred pounds. A light rain was falling as he walked up to the fence and struck his tongue out to touch the electric wire. We saw the sparks and heard the pop when his tongue touched the wire. He fell back on the ground then got up, bellowed and pawed the ground. Bully got mad and needed to attack something.

Bully, then turned and ran out in the pasture to Dad's prize apple tree standing alone in the field. Reaching the tree he began pushing and pushed it over till it was on the ground. We went running out there to save the tree, but it was down with Bully standing in the middle of the branches. Dad's prize innocent apple tree had been attacked, mortally wounded, and destroyed,

Friends, a bad temper will get you into unwanted situations. People will destroy good things when their temper gets a best of them. You have to learn to control your anger.

Take a deep breath and try to think about what has happened. Don't just react for that gets you in trouble. Bully just reacted and destroyed Dad's favorite apple tree. Learn to control your temper or you may destroy more than a tree.

FOOT ON THE RUDDER

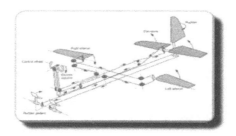

*E*very spring three of us would fly to the coast to go deep sea fishing. Both of my buddies had airplanes so getting there was no problem. I would meet them in Orangeburg a few miles from my house. Then we would take off for the coast. On this trip Keith was flying his plane and Chet was sitting in the back.

The weather was clear and beautiful as we took off. I was in the co-pilot seat. I would from time to time turn and talk with Chet in the backseat. I didn't realize that when I turned, my foot would mash the rudder pedal which made the plane go right.

Now, Keith was fighting to fly not knowing what was going on. I would turn to talk to Chet again and Keith fought to regain control of the plane. Checking everything in his mind for what the problem may be, he noticed it would happen when I turned to talk to Chet. He realized that when I turned I would mash the rudder petal pulling the plane to the right. He got my attention and told me to keep my foot off the rudder. From then on the flight was smooth.

Friends, if you put your foot on the rudder the plane will go right or left. You won't fly straight at all. That's true in life. If you set your mind on something and get sidetracked you'll end up off course. I've seen a young person have his or her life planned before they graduated from high school.

They have dreams to go to college and pursue a career. Then a marriage or baby, getting with the wrong crowd, and letting drugs and alcohol come into the picture and the direction of your life changes. Where they want to be is not where they are but off course. The dreams many times are lost. Keep your goals before you and your foot off the rudder.

DEEP SEA FISHING

eep sea fishing has always been a sport of mine. I try to go at least once a year. One of the first times I went was with a friend of mine, Reverend Jack Poole. We headed to Charleston and got on the boat. Now this was a large boat where fifty or sixty people were boarding to fish for the day.

We headed out and the water was a little choppy. Waves were running high. Riding along it's not bad but when the boat stops it really rocks and rolls. It wasn't long before most everyone was sick. Rev. Poole and I were just fine and started fishing. Rev. Poole had put in a chew of Red Man tobacco and was catching fish and spitting into the ocean.

All at once, something fell on him. As we looked at what it was, we recognized that it was bits of a hot dog. We looked up and on the upper deck was a lady and she said, "I am so sorry, I couldn't help it". Rev. Poole spit out his chew of Red Man tobacco and I noticed that he had lost his color. I asked him if he was alright and he said, "No, I need to go inside".

He went to the captain to tell him how sick he was. The captain told him to lie down in the cabin. Well, that didn't last long. Again he went to the captain offering to buy the boat so we could head to the shore. Rev. Poole was told that the boat would be out on the water for four more hours before heading into shore.

Then he begs the captain to sell him the boat so we could go ashore. By now, he was sick as a dog and he thought he was going to die. He didn't die, but that was the last deep sea fishing trip for him.

Friends, sometimes things just happen like bits of hot dogs falling from the sky. Rev. Poole would have been fine except for the lady losing her lunch on him. It is hard to prepare for things to go just right.

Things happen that you can't prepare for. Do the best you can and use your head when surprises happen. Sometimes the surprises are so surprising all you can do is endure the situation. That is what Rev. Poole had to do on our last deep sea fishing trip.

A PRAYER FOR LUNCH

*A*t my first appointment Rachael, my daughter, was five months old. A couple at the church adopted her as their granddaughter. Millie and Joe became her local grandparents. She would spend a lot of time with them even spending the night. They loved her so much.

After church on Sunday we would all go to lunch together and I was not allowed to pay for our lunch. We went to this cafeteria and it was always packed. It was a buffet style lunch. After each of us got our plates and sat down, Rachael said we had to pray. Now, she was about four years old at this time. Joe replied, "Go ahead honey, and pray".

She fixed her hands, bowed her head and said as loud as she could, "JESUS, BLESS THE FOOD AND BLESS MEMAW AND POPPY, AMEN". Now everything stopped when she prayed. The serving line stopped, people hushed talking and when she finished it was a great, 'Amen", in unison. Joe mumbled under his breath, "I won't ask her to pray anymore especially when everyone now knows my name is Poppy".

Friends, with that little prayer it stopped everything that day in the cafeteria. Many times it is the little things that change our lives. Think of a little virus and how it stopped the world in 2020. Rachael was sincere and everyone knew it and I believed God smiled. She was a great example for God. We should always try to be a good example for Him. Take time to say a prayer over your meal. You may never know how the little things will affect you or how a prayer over lunch could affect someone.

WHERE FIREWORKS GO

Mr. Marion was the pillar of this church I served. He was a quiet man with a strong faith. Also, he was a farmer in the community. One of his grandsons was a super intelligent little fellow named, Jared. When I would do children sermons on Sunday morning I had to really listen to Jared. His questions or answers were never simple and he put much thought into them.

Mr. Marion told me he needed to talk to me about something after church one Sunday. I agree to meet him on Monday morning at his home. It was at this time he told me this story. He said that he and Jared were checking the hogs (which he raised) and were now walking back to the house. It was the fourth of July and fireworks were heard throughout the community and hogs get nervous during loud noises.

Walking back to the house, Jared looked up at his granddad and said, "Granddaddy do you know where fireworks go when they go up into the air?" Knowing Jared, Mr. Marion replied, "No, I don't son, where do they go?" "They go to heaven." Jared responded. Mr. Marion replies, "They go to heaven?" "Yes, and when they get there the angels see them and say 'what in the hell was that'?" Now Jared was serious not trying to be funny or vulgar. This was the observation of a little seven year old boy.

Friends, children say some crazy things. Always listen to them. I know Jared's words have gone with me through the years. When I see fireworks being shot or a stand selling them I think of those angels. I picture these angels and hear them say, "What in the hell was that?" Now you know where those fireworks go.

STOPPING A HUNGRY MAN

$\mathcal{M}$y Dad would always cook something for our neighbors and friends every Saturday. On several occasions Dad would fry chitlins. These are large hog intestines that are cleaned, boiled, cut into links, and fried. In one of our small towns near where I live is the Sally's Chitlins Strut which is a big event every year the Saturday after Thanksgiving.

So Dad was frying them and once they were done, he would take them out to drain the grease off. One individual, Mr. Hungry Man, loved chitlins and could really eat his weight in them. He would eat them as fast as Dad could fry.

My brother, Jimmy, and I watched him and said, "We have got to stop him." We came up with the idea of going and getting some grains of corn (food of the hogs) and place them in some of the chitlins. Dad placed them in the grease and fried them golden brown. Of course Mr. Hungry Man was waiting and put some on his plate. "Boy, these are really good!" he remarked. We saw him stop chewing when he bit into one of those corn grains we had put in the uncooked chitlins before they were fried.

He moved the corn around in his mouth and then spit a piece of the grain out. He lost color in his face and set his plate down. He was through for the night and there were plenty of chitlins for the rest of us. When Dad wasn't looking we got those chitlins and my brother and I ate them. The mission was accomplished, so we ate our fill.

Friend, Mr. Hungry Man was a big man and could really eat. So we had to stop him. It may not have been the best plan but it worked. It's always hard to deal with situations like these. It is even harder to deal with people who are overbearing, controlling or a drama queen or king. Also, it is hard to change a person's characteristics with just words. I wish it was as easy as putting a piece of corn in hog intestines, but it's not. Sometimes it's best to just walk away.

CHANGING THE SONG

We met for the wedding rehearsal at six o'clock in the evening. Everyone to be present was present. The rehearsal went without a hitch. I asked the organist what song that the groom, best man and I would enter to take our places at the front. She told me and then we even practiced coming out on the song. Everything was on go for the wedding service.

The next day it was time for the service to start at seven o'clock. A few minutes before the time to start, I had prayer with the best man and the groom. We were ready to enter the sanctuary when the organist began to playing this song we had never heard. The organist kept planning but not the song for us to make our entrance

All at once the director came in and said "You're supposed to be out there." I said, "She hasn't played the song to enter." The director said that the organist had changed the song because she felt more comfortable with another one. "It would have been nice to have known that," I responded as we got ready to enter the sanctuary.

After the service I cornered the organist and said, "Why didn't you let me know you had changed the entering song?" She said that she forgot to inform me. I thought of some things to say but why? You can't fix stupid.

Readers, if you tell someone something, please stick with it. Don't change horses in midstream. If they don't know of the change it makes them look bad even though they are innocent. Now, that girl had an attitude which didn't help and even afterwards, she thought it was funny. It's at times like that I whisper, "Lord bless them with a brick." It may not be Christian but I am human too. Always keep your word to those you give it to and don't go changing the song.

THE RABBIT HUNT

*I*n an earlier story I told you about Thanksgiving at Aunt Maude's house. I mentioned about the yearly rabbit hunt for men and my cousins who were old enough. There were lots of rabbits around her house.

We had six beagles that were ready to go find a rabbit. We were stationed at different places for the hunt. The idea was for the beagles to run the rabbits to you. When the dogs were coming your way, get ready for a rabbit was running ahead of them.

This was my Cousin Billy's first hunt, so Uncle Smick stayed close to him. Uncle Smick stood at the bottom of a slab pile, which is the outer bark of a pine tree cut off by the saw mill. Then they would saw the lumber. These piles would be large and tall and made perfect homes for rabbits.

Billy was located away from the pile to intercept the rabbit first. The beagles were heading toward them and then there was the rabbit. Billy raised the gun to sight in on the rabbit and then he fired, Uncle Smick was in the line of fire. The shot hit him in the foot and lower leg. The rabbit was safe now in the slab pile.

They got a truck and came and got Uncle Smick and brought him to the house where everyone had gathered. They had heard he was shot but didn't know how bad. Aunt Dot, his wife, was thinking the worst. When Uncle arrived everything calmed down when they saw him. The family wanted to know what happened.

Uncle Smick simply said, "Billy was aiming at the rabbit, shot and missed him hitting me". They took him to the doctor in Swansea, a small town, and the doctor picked out the shot and bandaged him up. He was good to go.

Friends, be careful shooting a gun. Make sure you look behind your target to see what's there, especially if you hunt in the woods. You may hit something you didn't want to hit.

Hunting rabbits you have to shoot fast because they are running full speed. Yet look at the area you are shooting in and use some common sense. If you don't you may miss the rabbit and hit what you didn't want to hit.

SAVING KEITH

A group of us went to the Bahamas on a cruise. Among the group was a dear friend Keith, an attorney and now a judge. His wife and mine were also aboard, but Keith and I hung together.

While in the islands we went to this resort area with a beautiful beach. Now the waves down there are not like Myrtle Beach. The waves at Myrtle Beach roll in, while the waves in the Bahamas seem to roll and dive straight down.

Keith and I were ready to tackle the waves. Wearing our bathing suits we waded in. All at once a wave hit us and knocked us down. I got up but Keith was still down. Matt came to his rescue. I grabbed him to pull him up but he seemed to fight against me. Determined to save him I tried to pull him to his feet. Finally, he was able to speak and said, "No, don't pull me up my bathing suit is knocked down." The wave had knocked his bathing suit down. Now, I know why he was fighting me while I was determined to save him.

Readers, things may not always be what they seem. I was going to save Keith and he didn't want to be saved, until his trunks were up. In spite of my best efforts he wanted to stay down. If I were in his situation I would have fought me too.

Try to get the complete story before you decide what to do. I could have asked, "Are you alright?" then he could have shaken his head, yes. Don't just jump into something it may be like trying to save Keith.

HELPFUL NEIGHBOR

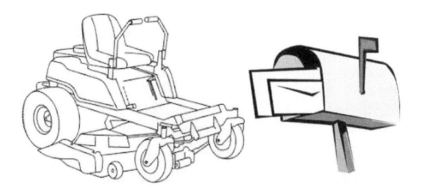

*A*fter my heart surgery I was very limited in what I could do. The surgeon told me to take it easy and I ended up having a lot of bed and chair time.

One day I was sitting on my back steps when my neighbor, Dickie, came over to check in on me. He mentioned the grass needed cutting so he asked if he could cut it for me. I thought this was a wonderful gesture to do for me. He had just bought a new zero-turn lawnmower and was learning to handle it properly.

Hearing the mower fire up I kept thinking what a nice thing to do for me. He started cutting in the front yard out of my sight. Then I hear Dickie coming around the house to the back yard. Coming into sight I see him on the lawn mower with my mailbox and pole in his hand. "Got a little too close to the mailbox," he said throwing it on the ground by me. My whole attitude changed and now I am wondering what else I could lose. It was such a relief when I heard the mower shut down next door. Another neighbor put the box back up for me the next day.

Friends, sometimes a good deed goes south. It doesn't always turn out like we want it to when friends help. Things will happen not because they planned it, they just happen. No use to get mad and throw a hissy fit, but just deal with it. Anger doesn't help or change the situation. Learn to laugh and move on to the next event. It will occur even with a helpful neighbor.

GETTING CAUGHT

I had just moved to my new church. Now this church had a security system, my first church with one. They instructed me on how to arm and disarm the system. I thought I was ready.

It was time for me to set up my office in the church. It was Wednesday morning and I headed across the road to the church. I unlocked the door and walked in and started putting books on the shelf in my new office. All of a sudden the alarm goes off. I run to the box and I couldn't remember the code. When they instructed me on the code, I remember it was under some bench, but I couldn't remember which bench.

The phone rings and I answer it. They ask me some questions and I tried to answer but I guess they were wrong. The lady on the other end of the line hangs up and I think I'll go get my wife and she can shut it down. Then all of a sudden sirens were hurting my ears.

As I left the church a sheriff's deputy had driven up. He gets out with hand on his revolver. "Who are you?" he asked. "I'm the new preacher, I just moved in," I answered. "Is that so," he replied. "Well, I know that they have a husband and wife here as ministers, so who are you?' Show me some identification," he said. "I left my billfold at the house right across the road," I told him. "I need to see some identification or I'll have to take you in," he said with his hand still on the gun.

About that time a church member drove up after hearing the alarm. "I see you have met our new preacher," Duwayne said. The deputy shook my hand and then drove off. Duwayne went in and shut the alarm off.

I was at this church for six years and not once did I ever go into the church without someone to disarm the alarm. Friends would drop by and say, "Let's have a look at your church?" I would respond, "No, I can't get pass the alarm system." I was the only minister in the state of South Carolina, who couldn't get into his own church. Thank God that my wife could.

Sometimes bad experiences affect us in the future. Such was this situation concerning the alarm. I chose not to get involved in disarming the alarm. I should have tried to learn more about the alarm system so I could have mastered it. It only affected me for six years.

I still remember that day when I saw the deputy standing there with his hand on his gun was a vision I never will forget. If Duwayne hadn't driven up I would have gone to jail, the first day of my new church. You see the deputy caught me.

A FALL SATURDAY

I n the fall a Saturday was about the same during most of the winter months. The big chore was the feeding of the animals. At day break the day began with loading of the corn on the truck.

This corn was broken early and stored in the shuck in the barn. After loading it we then grabbed our burlap bags to place the feed in and headed to Swansea. We pulled up to the Swansea Milling Company to grind the corn. We get in line to have our corn processed for the animals.

I can still hear that old mill mourn as it grinds the feed, and still smell the scent of ground corn in the air. The air really got sweet when they added the molasses to the mixture. Our turn came and they processed our load which was ground and placed in the burlap sacks. The mill operator thanked us and we headed across the road to pay.

They had all kinds of supplies and a water drink box. Drinks were placed in there and they were ice cold. Dad would tell me to get one. I reached into that cold water and grabbed a small Coke. Dad would get one too and we paid Mr. Smith for two drinks at ten cents per drink. That was the highlight of my day.

We arrived back at home and unloaded the feed and fed the cows to be butchered for winter meat. It was time for lunch and a big pot of dry lima beans had been cooking on the wood stove since early that morning. They smelled so good and were good when eaten with a piece of corn bread.

The day was full of chores and it was time to go hunt after the wood was gathered for the night. Hunting for rabbit or squirrel would provide Sunday dinner or a raccoon killed the night before. The day was over unless we went coon hunting that night.

Before going to bed the fire was always given more wood to burn slow during the night. Standing by the heater we would warm up as much as we could stand and then high tail it to the bed and jump in which had so much cover, it was hard to turn over.

Things were a lot simpler back then. No busy schedule just a simple pace for the day. Today the pace is ridiculous. Take time to just relax and take it easy. You won't have to grind feed but you can enjoy a Coke or Pepsi with a friend on Saturday.

RAY GOES DOWN

It was annual conference for the United Methodist at Wofford College. This is when each Methodist church in South Carolina sends a representative and their minister to adopt the agenda for the following year.

I was the representative from my home church, Ray was from the neighboring church and Reverend Poole was the minister of both churches. The three of us load up to ride to Wofford College together to attend the Methodist Conference.

Our lodging was at the college in dorm rooms. Rev. Poole and Ray roomed together and I was in the next room to them. Rev. Poole and I sat down to relax, but Ray was on a health kick so he went out to run on the college track.

The room had these large closets and I could stand up in it without any problem. Now this gave me an idea of scaring Ray. While Ray was gone I got a sheet and got in the closet. Placing the sheet over me I was ready. Ray came in out of breath and headed to the closet to get a towel. When he opened the door I jumped out and said, "Boo." Ray grabbed his chest and fell back across his bed. Rev. Poole shouted, "You're killed Ray, he's having a heart attack!"

Well, Ray got his breath and he didn't die, thank God. Yet when he would have to go in his closet he would look for me and then carefully open it up. By the way, Ray gave up the health kick after that episode.

Friends, you know I could have killed Ray. Thank God he's alive today and we still laugh about that day. Yet there are other things that can kill our spirit. A family member, a mate, children, a friend, or the loss of a pet can kill your spirit. They can hurt you so deeply with words or actions. Just remember to hold your head up and keep on walking. You may go down but you won't get knocked out.

KING AND THE SQUIRREL

Every year the pecans ripen and begin falling. The trees are in the back yard and the squirrels begin to eat the nuts. To get to the trees they have to cross a road. Once in the backyard they are safe jumping from tree to tree. The only danger is the road.

My dog, King, tries to catch them when they are on the ground. For a month or so he would try but always came up short. The squirrels would come down the tree and bark at him. Everyday this would happen and King would run after them.

One day the wind was blowing as the squirrels jumped from tree to tree. All of a sudden a squirrel jumped to a limb but the wind blew it out of the way. He hit the ground like a rock, stunning him for a few seconds and that was just enough time for King to catch him.

Now, that was one proud dog as King walked around with the squirrel in his mouth. If you tried to take it from him he would growl. He carried that squirrel around several days. He seemed to be so proud of finally catching one.

Friends, there are some things in life that are hard to do. You put a lot of energy in trying to get it done. Don't quit, keep on trying. Be patient and success will come with time. Don't get mad or frustrated along the way. It took Edison over a thousand times before he invented the light bulb.

Someone asked him, "Why don't you quit after all the failures?" Thomas Edison replied, "They aren't failures just ways to not do it." Great things are ahead for you, if you make your failures something positive and like King you will catch a squirrel.

MY WIFE ANGELA

My first marriage ended in a divorce, something I couldn't prevent. As she said, "I have to find herself." I had been training as a Hospital Chaplain during the separation and ultimately the divorce. I met Angela while at the hospital and we became friends.

Finishing up the chaplaincy I took a church again and it was then that our relationship began to develop. We were married and as my Mom said, "This time you got a good one." I concurred a 100 percent with Mom. Let me share with you why.

First of all she is my fashion consultant. I get dressed and come out and she will say, "That tie doesn't go with that shirt." She can also spot a spot on my shirt from across the room.

Second, she is my nurse. When I have had surgery she is right there. When I come home she makes sure I have everything I need. She is always there to help in my recovery. She is my nurse.

Third, she is my secretary. Angela types my sermons and funeral eulogies as I write them. She also typed my manuscript for the books I have written. I couldn't have done it without her. She is a computer whiz and my secretary.

Fourth, she is my spiritual aide. She drives me to religious functions, hospitals, and members' homes. Her faith is so strong and I cherish our night time talks in bed at the close of the day. I have supported her in her problems and she has been there for me. She is my spiritual aide.

Fifth, she is my wife. I cherish her presence and miss her so when she has to leave to go to her Mom's home. It's always good to see her come home again. I love her so. The way I look at her is in her name. if you take the 'a' off of Angela you have angel. Now that is what I believe God has given to me, my angel.

MS. DOTTIE

*I*t was a Sunday morning when Ms. Dottie's son, Hayne, approached me after church. His Mom was to have a biopsy but she refused. She was 94 and felt she didn't want to know what the result would be. Hayne wanted me to try and talk her into having it done.

Now, Ms. Dottie was one of those people who would tell you how she felt and what she thought of you. She wouldn't hold back. I told her son that if she had her mind made up I couldn't change it. Hayne said, "Just go and try."

Calling her that afternoon I set up to see her Monday morning. On arriving she met me at the door with her dog, Lucky. Ms. Dottie told the dog to leave me alone. After hugging her we both sat down in the den. She was in her recliner chair and I sat on the sofa next to her.

Lucky had crawled toward me on the floor and Ms. Dottie shouted, "Lucky, Damn you, leave the Preacher alone!" Turning to me she said, "I'm sorry, Preacher for cussing." Picking up our conversation, Lucky moved again on his belly toward me. "Damn you Lucky, I told you to leave the Preacher alone," she shouted! Again she apologized. This went on until Lucky climbed up on the couch next to me and his head touching my leg. By the way, she informed me that she wasn't going to have that biopsy.

There was a lull in our conversation and then she started coming up in her chair. I leaned over toward her. "You know one thing Preacher?" She asked. "What is it Ms. Dottie?" I responded. "You have to be tuff as hell, to grow old," she replied. I never forgot those words especially as I have grown older. People talk of the golden years. Yet, I haven't found them. The words of Ms. Dottie are very profound and true. Make the most of your time on earth before you grow old.

Matthew Rucker

LOSING A LEG

I have diabetes and one of my medicines caused a bone infection in my foot. Over the next five years I would fight the infection with the help and support of my great doctors; Dr. J. Kerns, Dr. W. Moore, Dr. N. Cauthen, and Dr. M. Barwick. In the process I had two toes and two knuckles amputated. A part of this five year journey was lots of IV and oral antibodies.

The straw that broke the camel's back was cutting open the bottom of my foot and then another round of IV's. It had been a long battle and I was tired so I said, "Cut it off".

Now in my mind, I thought taking it off and getting an artificial leg, I would be walking with no pain. Everything would be great. Boy was I wrong.

First of all you have to learn to walk again. Walking is not like it was before the surgery. It's totally different.

Second and most important is a rascal called 'phantom pain'. I remember my great aunt that had to have a leg removed. Sometimes she would sit in the wheel chair and rub her knee. I remembered asking her if her knee itched. She would reply, "No, it's my foot that hurts". I thought to myself that Aunt Carrie was losing it mentally, because how could your foot hurt when you have no foot. I never really understood that until July 15, 2019.

Sometimes the phantom pain is so great that I rub my knee. There is no foot but I feel the pain in my big toe. It's real, my friends, it's real. Every time I feel the pain my mind wanders back to Aunt Carrie rubbing her knee and say, "My foot hurts".

Life can throw some wicked curves at you. Changes come in life and things change factors such as death of a loved one, a broken relationship, an illness or surgery. When these things happen and they will, we need to come up with a new direction in life. This is hard to do but we have to if we are going to survive. So hold up your head, take a deep breath and learn to crawl then walk again. Hold on to your faith and keep moving forward for a new plan will come. Like me, hang in there.

WANDERING BACK

*W*ell, I am coming to the end of this book, sitting on my porch under a tin roof. The rain is falling and the sound is so beautiful. I truly am at home again, my birth place. As I sit here listing to the rain, my mind goes back to another time and place. Back when things were a lot simpler, some fifty seven years ago.

In my mind I see a hay field and a young boy throwing bales up on an old wooden wagon. The wagon is hooked to a hay baler pulled by a tractor. Standing on the front of the wagon I catch the bales that are coming out of the baler. Somedays we would bale over a thousand bales of hay for a dairy farm. It was owned by Barbara and Roger Hill.

We would break for lunch and Barbara would bring us a double cheeseburger and a gallon of tea for lunch. Now I would eat my fill and have to get back on that hay wagon. The temperature was around hundred degrees after lunch. Each wagon would hold around one hundred and twenty bales. This was my summer job.

I remember on one occasion the wagon was loaded and the bales had not been tied down yet with a rope. Coming out the hay field, we started down a small hill. So for some reason, maybe to slow the tractor down, Roger applied the brakes on the tractor. The load on the wagon separated and I am on the front, so here I go. Crawling out from under the hay bales, I am okay. Yet this was the only time that I could have killed Roger.

Working in the hot summer was a blessing in another way. I was ready for football practice. Others players would fall out but not me. 'Let's go' was my motto and I looked good! Almost like a bronze god with my tan.

Now you may ask, 'Why this story'? Well, there's a song sung by Bobby Bare entitled, '*Things Change*' and I borrowed two lines from the song.

Which stays; Things change don't bat your eye,

Things change they'll pass you buy.

The rain is coming down harder now, as my mind stays back in the past, walking through the rows of my field of memories. As the rain increases I think of that hay field. You know it doesn't seem that long ago, but things have changed. Life doesn't stand still, it keeps on moving. So keep moving for one day you may be sitting on a porch with the rain falling thinking of you years ago. 'And you know what?' It won't seem so long ago.

EPILOGUE

. . . .

I have lived a full life, traveled to exotic places and met interesting people. It has been a good life, in spite of some setbacks such as divorce, suicide of a son, and health problems. All in all though, I have many memories, in a field of memories. I have shared with you some of my stories and hope that they have been meaningful. The aim was to show my love of God, my love of people and that I was a bit of a rascal. Sharing my Field of Memories maybe you have gained some wisdom and joy. I moved from the springtime of my life as a young boy, then to middle age and now the fall of my life, old age.

Now, what can we say about old age? We want to keep death at bay. "No closer, leave me alone," we cry. Exercise, vitamins, and the right diet will keep it away. I even had one church member tell me he wasn't going to grow old, but he did and I buried him. Growing old however, is not for sissies.

I sit here with an amputated leg. On the good leg I had surgery and now injections to try to make it strong enough for me to walk again. I'm trying to walk on an artificial leg and its hard learning to walk. I battle diabetes and live in pain and things that I've done all my life I can't do. It's like being in a virtual prison.

The picture on the front of the book with my granddaughter is taken in a field of crimson clover on our farm. This book's title *'A Field Of Memories'*, where each of us are making our own memories, both good and bad. Some are as fresh as yesterday while others, go back a lifetime. Each of you is building a field of memories from birth to death. Everyone has memories and stories to share. Take time to share them with family and friends.

So I am going through the golden years holding on to my faith. May God bless each of you as you make your *Field of Memories.*